Keto Slow Cooker Recipes

Life-Changing Guide To Ketogenic Diet Recipes For Your Slow Cooker That You Can Cook At Home

TABLE OF CONTENTS

Introduction

Even though there are many diets and trends, also very few diets, still remain vastly popular, both for their weight loss efficiency as well as long-term health benefits. The Ketogenic diet (or Keto diet in brief) is a relatively new diet pattern that has taken the world by storm and it's no wonder why.

Ketogenic diet's philosophy, as we'll examine in more detail in a later chapter, is a low-carb high-fat diet rich in healthy fats. Through a process called "ketosis", the diet utilizes fats to generate energy and this, in turn; burns excess body fat and lowers the risk of developing inflammatory disorders like diabetes or heart disease. This is why it is often suggested by doctors globally to patients that suffer from these problems.

The best part of following a Ketogenic diet while using your Slow Cooker is that you don't need to do extravagant stuff or buy fancy ingredients or supplements to prepare Keto-friendly and delicious meals. All you need to know is a few basic things such as how it works, what to eat, and what to avoid. This isn't a very restrictive diet and it won't take you much time to adjust as healthy fats will replace most if not all your sweet and carb cravings eventually.

"Ketogenic", "Keto", "Ketosis" or even "High Fat/Low Carb" diet is a diet pattern that involves the consumption of fats in high amounts and the limited consumption of carbs. The primary purpose of the Ketogenic diet is to produce ketone bodies in the liver, which will later serve as the body's primary fuel and energy source. This process is called "ketosis" and is considered to be a normal metabolic process in the body for generating energy.

The philosophy behind the Ketogenic diet stems from the fact that our bodies either need glucose or fats to generate energy. The typical western diet, which is rich in carbs and sugars, utilizes these components as the main energy source within our systems. These are often found in sweets, starches, gluten bread, sodas/fizzy drinks and processed food meals.

The system either receives these and breaks them down into simple sugars to generate energy or stores them in the liver and muscle tissue in the form of glycogens. However, relying only on carbs and glucose to generate energy may lead to various health problems in the long run associated with inflammation like diabetes, heart problems, and even cancer.

Ketogenic diet essentially can replace the need of carbs and glucose as the main energy fuel with healthier fats. Whenever our systems can't find any glucose to generate energy, they will seek alternative means to do that. In particular, in the case of "ketosis", the body starts to break down fat deposits to release glucose from triglycerides. So through the process of ketosis, our bodies are "forced" in a right way to produce ketone acids which attack burn off deposited fat cells.

It may sound weird to some, but in this case, it takes fat to lose fat - a high fatty diet can actually lead to weight loss and other health benefits, both temporary and long-term.

Now, even though the Keto diet calls for high amounts of fat, it doesn't eliminate other foods like protein for example, which should also be taken in balance. A low dose of carbs should still be taken when following a Keto diet. Most guides and nutritional experts recommend this proportion of macros:

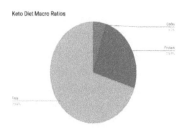

The above is one of the most popular Ketogenic diet proportions, but there are slight variations of this like for example the Keto plan that implements 80% fats, 15% of protein and only 5% fat. In general though, in all Ketogenic meal plans fats consist 70-80% of the diet macros, whereas protein comes second by 15-30% and carbs, of course, are the least to be consumed eating only up to 10% of the total macro intake.

The Ketogenic diet is also broken down into further categories based on exercise and weight loss plans. Here are the main three:

Standard Keto Diet. This is the most popular Ketogenic diet form. This requires 20 to 50 grams of carbs per day taken anytime during the day.

Targeted Keto Diet. This is a Ketogenic diet that is mostly favored by athletes and bodybuilders for the purpose of lean muscle enhancement and energy improvements. This also calls for the consumption of 20 to 50 grams of carbs per day but this should be taken ideally one hour before working out.

Cyclical Keto Diet. This is the most flexible form of a Keto diet as it involved eating a low amount of carbs most days e.g. 5% followed by a couple of days of consuming more amounts of carbs e.g. 15%.

Now, even though Keto diet is actually a low carb/ high-fat diet, it has a few key differences with popular low carb diets like Atkins. These kinds of diets tend to contain a higher amount of carbs in specific periods which are not enough to trigger "ketosis" in the body. Some of these diets also have lower amounts of fat and higher amounts of fiber to help weight loss. Still, Ketogenic diet is superior to these for the numerous other health benefits it offers besides just weight loss.

The thing is, when the system is used to a diet rich in carbs, it takes some time to adjust to a Keto diet but this typically lasts only a few days or a couple of weeks. Some folks experience symptoms like flu-like signs, headaches, nausea, and dizziness during the brief stage of transition. These are triggered due to the system suddenly getting deprived of carbs, which were formerly used to fuel the brain but they typically vanish as your body gets used to "ketosis".

Even though "ketosis" doesn't develop at the same speed and point for everyone, on average, it takes 2-3 days for the system to initiate ketosis. If you want to test your ketone levels and confirm that your body is a state of ketosis there are actually some quick and handy methods to do it at home. For example:

Using a urine strip to measure ketone levels in your urine

Using a blood glucose measuring tool

Using a breath meter

The most accurate of these three is considered to be the blood glucose tool. Urine testing is more practical than blood testing but tends to offer less accurate results. Still, these tools are optional and you don't need them when following a Ketogenic program as you'll most likely experience any changes yourself.

The Health Advantages of Keto Diet

Even though no diet is perfect when it comes to working for everyone, Keto diet is one of the few diet patterns that bear positive effects in our waistline and health--from trimming down body fat to even helping Epilepsy and Alzheimer's.

In brief, there is evidence that Ketogenic diet may be the most suitable diet to help people suffering from the following conditions:

Diabetes (I & 11)

Elevated blood pressure

High Cholesterol

Chronic Inflammation

Obesity

High Blood Sugar

Heart disorders

Fatty Liver Disease

Epilepsy

Alzheimer's

Parkinson's disease

Cancer

On a more general level, people who follow a Ketogenic diet long-term may notice the following benefits:

Improved energy and stamina

Better weigh control

Better mental clarity and focus

Decrease in inflammation that triggers various health problems.

Before we explain these benefits in more detail, let's examine first why such benefits occur and what are the deep benefits of following a keto diet from a cellular perspective. As mentioned in an earlier chapter, carbs and sugars are usually the primary sources of fuel for our systems to function. However, when these are deprived, our bodies automatically seek alternative sources to generate energy and in this case, it's fats creating ketone bodies.

However, whenever our systems use sugars/carbs to generate fuel, this causes a series of "reactive oxygen species". These nasty guys here trigger inflammation, destruction, and even cell death when they become out of control. This the reason why sugar and carbs are so unpopular and unhealthy - they can actually make you fat and dumb!

On the contrary, ketones provide a healthier and more sustainable fuel source that actually prevents the damage and inflammation of cell membranes and neurons in the brain tissue. This is partially due to the fact that ketone bodies control the devastating effects of reactive oxygen reactions and actually help support cellular and mitochondrial function and repair.

Now the healthy cells that are deprived of carbs (as their primary energy source) will automatically switch to a self-cleaning mode to survive and clear all their junk. This process is also known as "autophagy". This is a crucial procedure that controls many functions that make-up cellular health and flexibility and clean up the cell from damage and inflammation.

This ideal mix of ketone bodies and autophagy is what helps people suffering from cancer, brain disorders, and heart problems improve.

In short, Ketogenic diet produces the following benefits on a cellular and body level:

Ketone bodies are burned off faster and more efficiently compared to sugar/carbs

Limited consumption of carbs triggers cell autophagy (cell cleansing) and fight for inflammation and damage

Using ketones as a fuel source generates fewer reactive oxygen species

For the body:

Insulin levels start to drop as there are not enough carbs to trigger its release

Fat burning is stimulated because the system uses alternative energy sources and burns deposited fat for this.

Inflammatory disorders or the risk of developing such disorders is reduced.

CHAPTER 1:

Keto Diet & Slow Cooker Basics

I n the simplest of terms, a ketogenic diet is a very low-carb, high-fat diet. It isn't a new diet, either. It was created in the 1920s as a treatment for children who had epilepsy. It is still used today, but there has been more investigation to see if it is a breakthrough treatment for several other diseases and neurological disorders. So, this isn't just some weight loss trend.

The main goal is to place the body into ketosis. The body burns carbs as energy. But if the amount of carbs in the body is restricted, the body will start breaking down the fat stored within the body, and this will create what is known as ketones. These ketones are then used as fuel.

Move from the 1920s; researchers started to find that the keto diet provided benefits other than the control of epilepsy. Many wellness professionals, the world over, are embracing the word ketogenic. Many people have started using this diet to control and prevent diabetes and to lose weight.

Many studies have found that the ketogenic diet and other low-carb diets are perfect for losing weight. They tend to work better than a low-fat or reduced-calorie diet. The ketogenic diet is sometimes easier to follow because ketones can work as an appetite suppressant without consuming many carbohydrates; you aren't faced with sugar crashes or cravings for carbs. You eat plenty of fat to keep you feeling full.

What Are the Benefits?

Below are some of the benefits of ketones:

Weight Loss – The body has to burn fat to make ketones. When this happens, natural ketosis is going to cause weight loss. Some studies suggest ketones can help you lose weight while also curbing your appetite.

Diabetes Control – Many low-carb diets, like the keto diet, have been found to do a great job at lowering blood sugar levels and insulin resistance. Some studies have found that BHB ketone can reduce inflammation, which is another way to control diabetes.

Longevity – If you want to stay healthy and live a long life, occasionally fasting can help you do that. Studies have found that restricting carbs can help to lengthen your life expectancy.

Preventing Cancer – Glucose can increase cancer cells. When you don't let them have their favorite food, it can reduce cancer cells and help prevent and treat cancer. Many who are at risk of developing cancer or being treated for cancer will follow a ketogenic diet.

Resilience – Ketone bodies can provide your body with powerful and constant energy. They can also help to preserve your performance and stability better than glucose ever could.

Brainpower – The ketogenic diet was initially meant to be an epilepsy treatment, but it has been found as a great way to protect the neurons in the brain. It can improve focus, mental energy, and create a sharper mind.

Slow Cooker Basics

Having a slow cooker is an effortless, fast, and most flexible cooking method at any home. It didn't require you any cooking skills; it saves your time as the slow cooker does all the working time for you, truly safe and can even be used in any places like a hotel room or even student dorm as they possess a kettle like-shape, making it more portable than a stove. So, in the following guides, we will be talking some of the helpful basic ways to guarantee that you get the best out of your slow cooker.

What is it?

The slow cooker appeared in 1970 and was marketed as a bean cooker. But as it was modified, people started to use it to heat food and keep it warm for prolonged periods. And look how far we've come; people are cooking delicious healthy meals in it. It is a perfect small kitchen appliance that consists of a glass lid, porcelain, or a ceramic pot (it is inside of the heating unit) and, of course, a heating element. The modern

Slow Cooker could be of an oval or round shape and various sizes, from small to large. All the Slow Cookers have two settings: LOW (it corresponds to the temperature of 200°F mostly) and HIGH (up to 300°F). The WARM selection that is among the majority of the slow cookers' options nowadays allows keeping the prepared dishes warm for a long time. Some of the Slow Cooker models have a timer that will enable you to control cooking time if you are busy.

The Cooking Utensils Needed

First of all, you will need a Slow Cooker. Even though most models make a range of good varieties, you need to make sure you chose the slow cooker that meets your requirement.

You need to have a chopping board and at least three knives: a paring knife, a chef's knife, and a cleaver. Combining these knives will make it easy to prepare your foods, from herbs to full fleshed chickens.

You will also need a few bowls. These are important if you are going to be doing any mixing, preparing your ingredients in advance, or if you will need to take out some food from the cock-pot to make room for more ingredients.

You will also need a blender for smooth soups, a pestle and mortar if you want to crush your fresh herbs and spices, and a whisk for mixing eggs and sauces. Although these are not necessities, they will make the cooking process much more manageable if present. But in cases where you will be doing some batch cooking, consider investing in some good quality, resilient Tupperware. That way, you will make a great batch of food in advance and refrigerate them for future use.

If you intend to cook shorter recipes while you are out and about, you will either need a Slow Cooker or a Slow cooker with a timer, or a plug adapter with a timer built into it. In as much as the Slow Cooker are safe, it is inadvisable to leave your food on high pressure for eight to ten hours, as not only will it be an irresponsible act, but will most certainly ruin your food. In other words, timers are essential when cooking in absentia.

The Cooking Precautions

Even though Slow Cooker cooking is incredibly safe, it is recommended that you should always be careful:

- Do not place the slow cooker close to the pot or its wires as this could cause a hazard.

- Do not leave the house if your slow cooker is on without setting a safe timer.

- Do not leave the slow cooker exposed within reach of children or animals.

- Do not leave the slow cooker on with nothing inside it.

- Do not place the slow cooker on an unstable surface.

- Do not leave foods in it when cooked and cooled, as this can be dangerous to your health. Always move the cooked foods to a refrigerator or freezer for storage.

- And always make sure to follow these safety guidelines.

- Always make sure your slow cooker is clean.

- Always make sure your slow cooker is turned off when not in use.

- Always put your slow cooker somewhere safe and steady when not in use.

- Always follow the manufacturer's directions during usage, cleaning, and storage processes.

What Are the Benefits of Using the Slow Cooker?

What is the most difficult thing for you in the kitchen? You waste too much time in the kitchen when you might go to the cinema with friends? Do you spend too much money on products, and your ideas on what to prepare today are running out? The solution to all your problem? It is the Slow Cooker!

Firstly, it is possible to prepare meals when you are not at home. During those hectic family mornings, throw all the ingredients together following the recipe, switch the machine on, and go work.

Secondly, you don't like washing the dishes? Just clean the Slow Cooker and the plates after delicious meals. That's all! Using the Slow Cooker means having fewer dishes to wash.

Thirdly, the Slow Cooker cooks' delicious meals and saves your money!

These meals taste even better than usual, and also you can keep the leftovers in the refrigerator to eat afterward. How perfect are the spice flavors if you eat the dishes right after cooking! You might taste the cayenne pepper, cumin, ginger, and other favorite spices of yours. Buy simple products and follow the cookbook. It is easy!

The fourth benefit, the Slow Cooker, is the best way to keep your meal tender and always warm.

Fifth, the Slow Cooker reduces calories and fat. No oil (just olive or avocado oil), no frying is necessary.

Six is the step by step preparation.

Step by step preparation facilitates everyday cooking, especially for those who are not great fans of this process. In most recipes, all the ingredients are added at one time to the Slow Cooker.

Seven, it is energy saving. It requires less electricity than the regular oven.

The flexibility of the Slow Cooker is benefit number eight. You can take it on a trip, put it on the kitchen table or somewhere else. It doesn't need that much space.

And finally, benefit number nine is in the large quantities of prepared meals. Most of these recipes make large quantities of the end products, so you may feed an entire family and even freeze for tomorrow to make easy and quick lunches or suppers.

CHAPTER 2:

Slow Cooker Tips & Tricks

I f you have ever tossed a bunch of different ingredients into your Slow Cooker in the morning and thought about how delicious your dinner was going to be all day long, only to come home to a pot of mush, you might feel like giving up. However, don't give up just yet. Here are the top tips and tricks that you can use to ensure you are the master of your Slow Cooker in no time flat:

Start with frozen meat, that it at room temperature. Itis because you do want to brown the outside of the beef in advance; before you put it in your slow cooker. When you caramelize the outside of the meat, you are going to get a deep, delicious flavor in your dish. It also suggested that when you do brown the heart, you do so only after you have seasoned it. It will create a fantastic flavor.

Don't forget about the brown bits. The brown bits are the tiny morsels that are left in the pan after the meat has browned. They are packed full of flavor. You will want them in your Slow Cooker. You can deglaze your pan by adding some stock, water, or even wine to the pan. Cook over medium heat while carefully scraping the browned bits off of the bottom of the pan with a wooden spoon. Most of these are going to dissolve that you can use to make a nice sauce.

If you do use wine in your Slow Cooker, don't cook with any wine that you would not drink. Each of your ingredients should be quality ingredients. The Slow Cooker is not a magic machine that is going to turn low-quality ingredients into a high-quality food. Imagine how bad a cake would taste if you used old poor-quality chocolate.

If you add tomatoes to your recipes, it is essential to choose tomatoes that are not going to turn out mushy. Choose whole canned tomatoes instead of crushed. If you want the tomatoes to be in smaller pieces, chop them up before you put them in the in your Slow Cooker. You can also use dried tomatoes but never do you want to use fresh tomatoes in your Slow Cooker. They will turn into mush.

Don't freak out if you look into the Slow Cooker and find that there is too much liquid. Transfer some of that liquid to a saucepan. You can make gravy out of it or use it to glaze the food.

If you open up your Slow Cooker and find that your meat is perfectly cooked, but your vegetables are overcooked, remove the vegetables that are overcooked. Never serve the dish with overcooked vegetables. Serve the meat with a side of freshly cooked vegetables. You can also puree the overcooked vegetables and mix them in with the sauce.

Make sure that you understand how your Slow Cooker works. The high setting is only used when cooking foods for a shorter time. You do not want to leave your Slow Cooker on the high setting for 10 or 12 hours because you are going to come back to a burned mess. Make sure that you always check to ensure you are using the right setting.

You will find that some of the foods that you make in your Slow Cooker are going to taste better the following day. It is because flavors have been able to develop as the food sits so many meat dishes and chilies are going to be better the day after you make them.

The great thing about Slow Cooker is that it works very well with fattier cuts of meat. When you cook them on low and for a long time, the fat is going to make sure that the meat will not become dry. Since fattier cuts are generally the cheaper cuts, this is a great thing when it comes to your budget. It doesn't mean that you should not cook lean meats in your Slow Cooker. It is okay for you to cook meats like chicken breast in the Slow Cooker, but it is advisable to do this on days when you know you are going to be around.

When you are using it, it is essential to make sure that the food you add to it is appropriately layered. Most of the time the source of heat will be at the bottom of the Slow Cooker. It means that you need to place foods on the bottom of the Slow Cooker that will take more time to cook, such as root vegetables, or severe cuts of meat. The more delicate vegetables should be at the top of the slow cooker or added within the last 30 minutes to ensure that they do not turn into mush.

Every time that you lift that lid, it will add about 30 minutes to the cooking time, so don't do it. Having a glass lid, it allows you to see how the food is doing. So, do not open the Slow Cooker until the end of the cooking time, then if you need to you can add other spices or ingredients.

Herbs and dairy should always be added at the end of the cooking process. You will only stir in items like sour cream right before you serve the dish. If you do this too early, the dairy product will curdle and ruin your entire plate.

Some vegetables that you add such as onions may add too much liquid to your recipe if you find this, remove the lid from the Slow Cooker for about 30 minutes and turn it on high. It is going to boil off the extra liquid.

Not all Slow Cooker is the same, so if while you are working through these recipes, you find that they are not cooking for the exact time that the recipe says they should it is okay. What that means is that your recipes may get done a bit sooner or a bit afterward than what the recipe says they will. It is only because all Slow Cooker is different. While others may run a bit hot, yours may take a bit longer to heat up. If you notice that one recipe takes a bit longer to cook or that most of the recipes do, make a note of that and then you will know in the future that you will need to add a bit more time when cooking in the Slow Cooker.

CHAPTER 3:

Breakfast

1. Cherry Tomatoes Thyme Asparagus Frittata

Difficulty: Very Easy

Preparation time: 15 minutes

Cooking time: 6 hours

Servings: 6

Ingredients:

- 2 tablespoons unsalted butter, ghee, or extra-virgin olive oil

- 12 large eggs

- ¼ cup heavy (whipping) cream

- 1 tablespoon minced fresh thyme

- ½ teaspoon kosher salt

- ¼ teaspoon freshly ground black pepper

- 1½ cups shredded sharp white Cheddar cheese, divided

- ½ cup grated Parmesan cheese

- 16 cherry tomatoes

- 16 asparagus spears

Directions:

1. Glaze the inside of the slow cooker with the butter.

2. In the slow cooker, beat the eggs, then whisk in the heavy cream, thyme, salt, and pepper.

3. Add ¾ cup of Cheddar cheese and the Parmesan cheese and stir to mix.

4. Sprinkle the remaining ¾ cup of Cheddar cheese over the top. Scatter the cherry tomatoes over the frittata.

5. Arrange the asparagus spears decoratively over the top. Cook within 6 hours on low or 3 hours on soaring. Serve.

Nutrition:

Calories: 370 Fat: 29g Carbs: 4g Protein: 24g

2. Healthy Low Carb Walnut Zucchini Bread

Difficulty: Very Easy

Preparation time: 15 minutes

Cooking time: 3 hours & 10 minutes

Servings: 12

Ingredients:

- 3 eggs

- 1/2 cup walnuts, chopped

- 2 cups zucchini, shredded

- 2 tsp vanilla

- 1/2 cup pure all-purpose sweetener

- 1/3 cup coconut oil, softened

- 1/2 tsp baking soda

- 1 1/2 Tsp baking powder

- 2 tsp cinnamon

- 1/3 cup coconut flour

- 1 cup almond flour

- 1/2 Tsp salt

Directions:

1. Mix the almond flour, baking powder, cinnamon, baking soda, coconut flour, and salt in a bowl. Set aside.

2. Whisk eggs, vanilla, sweetener, and oil in another bowl.

3. Put dry batter to the wet and fold well. Add walnut and zucchini and fold well.

4. Pour batter into the silicone bread pan. Place the bread pan into the slow cooker on the rack.

5. Cook on high within 3 hours. Cut the bread loaf into the slices and serve.

Nutrition:

Calories: 174 Fat: 15.4 g

Carb: 5.8 g Protein: 5.3 g

3. Savory Creamy Breakfast Casserole

Difficulty: Very Easy

Preparation time: 15 minutes

Cooking time: 6 hours Servings: 8

Ingredients:

- 1 tablespoon unsalted butter, Ghee

- 10 large eggs, beaten

- 1 cup heavy (whipping) cream

- 1½ cups shredded sharp Cheddar cheese, divided

- ½ cup grated Romano cheese

- ½ teaspoon kosher salt

- ¼ teaspoon freshly ground black pepper

- 8 ounces thick-cut ham, diced

- ¾ head broccoli, cut into small florets

- ½ onion, diced

Directions:

1. Grease the slow cooker with the butter.

2. Whisk the eggs, heavy cream, ½ cup of Cheddar cheese, the Romano cheese, salt, and pepper inside the slow cooker.

3. Stir in the ham, broccoli, and onion. Put the remaining 1 cup of Cheddar cheese over the top.

4. Cook within 6 hours on low or 3 hours on high. Serve hot.

Nutrition:

Calories: 465

Fat: 36g

Carbs: 7g

Protein: 28g

4. **Low-Carb Hash Brown Breakfast Casserole**

Difficulty: Very Easy

Preparation time: 15 minutes

Cooking time: 6 hours Servings: 6

Ingredients:

- 1 tablespoon unsalted butter, Ghee

- 12 large eggs

- ½ cup heavy cream

- 1 teaspoon kosher salt

- ½ teaspoon ground black pepper

- ½ teaspoon ground mustard

- 1 head cauliflower, shredded or minced

- 1 onion, diced

- 10 ounces cooked sausage links, sliced

- 2 cups shredded Cheddar cheese, divided

Directions:

1. Grease the slow cooker with the butter.

2. Beat the eggs, then whisk in heavy cream, 1 teaspoon of salt, ½ teaspoon of pepper, and the ground mustard in a large bowl.

3. Spread about one-third of the cauliflower in an even layer in the bottom of the cooker.

4. Layer one-third of the onions over the cauliflower, then one-third of the sausage, and top with ½ cup of Cheddar cheese. Season with salt and pepper. Repeat twice.

5. Pour the egg batter evenly over the layered ingredients, then sprinkle the remaining ½ cup Cheddar cheese on top—Cook within 6 hours on low. Serve hot.

Nutrition:

Calories: 523 Fat: 40g Carbs: 7g Protein: 33g

5. **Onion Broccoli Cream Cheese Quiche**

Difficulty: Very Easy

Preparation time: 15 minutes

Cooking time: 2 hours & 25 minutes

Servings: 8

Ingredients:

- 9 eggs

- 2 cups cheese, shredded and divided

- 8 oz cream cheese

- 1/4 Tsp onion powder

- 3 cups broccoli, cut into florets

- 1/4 Tsp pepper

- 3/4 Tsp salt

Directions:

1. Add broccoli into the boiling water and cook for 3 minutes. Drain well and set aside to cool.

2. Add eggs, cream cheese, onion powder, pepper, and salt in mixing bowl and beat until well combined.

3. Spray slow cooker from inside using cooking spray.

4. Add cooked broccoli into the slow cooker then sprinkle half cup cheese.

5. Pour egg mixture over broccoli and cheese mixture.

6. Cook on high within 2 hours and 15 minutes.

7. Once it is done, then sprinkle the remaining cheese and cover for 10 minutes or until cheese melted. Serve.

Nutrition:

Calories 296

Fat 24.3 g

Carb 3.9 g

Protein 16.4 g

6. **Delicious Thyme Sausage Squash**

Difficulty: Very Easy

Preparation time: 15 minutes

Cooking time: 6 hours

Servings: 4

Ingredients:

- 2 tablespoons extra-virgin olive oil

- 14 ounces smoked chicken sausage, thinly sliced

- 1/4 cup chicken broth

- 1 onion, halved and sliced

- 1/2 medium butternut squash, peeled, diced

- 1 small green bell pepper, strips

- 1/2 small red bell pepper, strips

- 1/2 small yellow bell pepper, strips

- 2 teaspoons snipped fresh thyme or ½ teaspoon dried thyme, crushed

- 1/2 teaspoon kosher salt

- 1/2 teaspoon freshly ground black pepper

- 1 cup shredded Swiss cheese

Directions:

1. Combine the olive oil, sausage, broth, onion, butternut squash, bell peppers, thyme, salt, and pepper in the slow cooker. Toss to mix. Cook within 6 hours on low.

2. Before serving, sprinkle the Swiss cheese over the top, cover, and cook for about 3 minutes more to melt the cheese.

Nutrition:

Calories: 502

Fat: 38g

Carbs: 12g

Protein: 27g

7. Mexican Style Breakfast Casserole

Difficulty: Very Easy

Preparation time: 15 minutes

Cooking time: 5 hours

Servings: 5

Ingredients:

- 5 eggs

- 6 ounces pork sausage, cooked, drained

- ½ cup 1% milk

- ½ teaspoon garlic powder

- 2 jalapeños, deseeded, finely chopped

- ½ teaspoon ground cumin

- ½ teaspoon ground coriander

- 1 ½ cups chunky salsa

- 1 ½ cup pepper Jack cheese, shredded

- Salt to taste

- Pepper to taste

- ¼ cup fresh cilantro

Directions:

1. Coat the slow cooker with cooking spray. Mix the eggs, salt, pepper, plus milk in a bowl.

2. Add garlic powder, cumin, coriander, and sausage and mix well.

3. Pour the mixture into the slow cooker. Set the slow cooker on 'Low' within 4-5 hours or on 'High' for 2-3 hours. Place toppings of your choice and serve.

Nutrition:

Calories: 320

Fat: 24.1 g

Carb: 5.2 g

Protein: 17.9 g

8. **Almond Lemon Blueberry Muffins**

Difficulty: Very Easy

Preparation time: 15 minutes

Cooking time: 3 hours

Servings: 3

Ingredients:

- 1 cup almond flour

- 1 large egg

- 3 drops stevia

- ¼ cup fresh blueberries

- ¼ teaspoon lemon zest, grated

- ¼ teaspoon pure lemon extract

- ½ cup heavy whipping cream

- 2 tablespoons butter, melted

- ½ teaspoon baking powder

Directions:

1. Whisk the egg into a bowl. Add the rest of the fixing, and mix.

2. Pour batter into lined or greased muffin molds. Pour up to ¾ of the cup.

3. Pour 6 ounces of water into the slow cooker. Place an aluminum foil at the bottom, and the muffin molds inside.

4. Set the slow cooker on 'High' within 2-3 hours. Let it cool in the oven for a while.

5. Remove from the cooker. Loosen the edges of the muffins. Invert on to a plate and serve.

Nutrition:

Calories: 223

Fat: 21g

Carb: 5g

Protein: 6 g

9. **Healthy Veggie Omelet**

Difficulty: Very Easy

Preparation time: 15 minutes

Cooking time: 1 hour & 40 minutes Servings: 4

Ingredients:

- 6 eggs

- 1 tsp parsley, dried

- 1 tsp garlic powder

- 1 bell pepper, diced

- 1/2 cup onion, sliced

- 1 cup spinach

- 1/2 cup almond milk, unsweetened

- 4 egg whites

- Pepper

- Salt

Directions:

1. Grease the slow cooker from inside using cooking spray.

2. Whisk egg whites, eggs, parsley, garlic powder, almond milk, pepper, and salt in a large bowl.

3. Stir in bell peppers, spinach, and onion. Pour egg batter into the slow cooker.

4. Cook on high within 90 minutes or until egg sets. Cut into the slices and serve.

Nutrition:

Calories: 200

Fat: 13.9 g

Carb: 5.8 g

Protein 13.4 g

10. **Arugula Cheese Herb Frittata**

Difficulty: Very Easy

Preparation time: 15 minutes

Cooking time: 3 hours & 10 minutes

Servings: 6

Ingredients:

- 8 eggs

- 3/4 cup goat cheese, crumbled

- 1/2 cup onion, sliced

- 1 1/2 cups red peppers, roasted and chopped

- 4 cups baby arugula

- 1 tsp oregano, dried

- 1/3 cup almond milk

- Pepper Salt

Directions:

1. Grease the slow cooker using a cooking spray. Whisk eggs, oregano, and almond milk in a mixing bowl.

2. Put pepper and salt. Arrange red peppers, onion, arugula, and cheese into the slow cooker.

3. Pour egg batter into the slow cooker over the vegetables. Cook on low within 3 hours. Serve hot and enjoy.

Nutrition:

Calories: 178

Fat: 12.8 g

Carb: 6 g

Protein: 11.4 g

CHAPTER 4:

Lunch

11. Fisherman's Stew

Difficulty: Medium

Preparation Time: 17 Minutes

Cooking Time: 8 Hours and 35 Minutes

Servings: 6

Ingredients:

- 2 tbsp. olive oil

- 2 garlic cloves, finely chopped

- 1 cup baby carrots, sliced 1/4 inch thick

- 6 large Roma tomatoes, sliced and quartered

- 1 green bell pepper, chopped

- 1/2 tsp. fennel seed

- 1 cup water

- 1 bottle (8 oz.) clam juice

- 1-pound cod, cut into 1-inch cubes

- 1/2-pound medium shrimp, uncooked, peeled, and deveined

- 1 tsp. sugar

- 1 tsp. dried basil leaves

- 1/2 tsp. salt

- 1/4 tsp. red pepper sauce

- 2 tbsp. fresh parsley, chopped

Directions:

1. Stir the olive oil, garlic, carrots, tomatoes, green pepper, fennel seed, water, and clam juice together in the slow cooker.

2. Cover then cook it for 8 to 9 hours on LOW. Vegetables should be tender.

3. Twenty minutes before serving, add cod, shrimp, sugar, basil, salt, and pepper sauce.

4. Cover and cook 15 to 20 minutes on HIGH. The soup is ready when the fish can easily be flaked and shrimp are pink in color. Serve and enjoy!

Nutrition:

Calories 180,

Fat 26,

Carbs 10,

Protein 10

12. **Pumpkin Chili**

Difficulty: Hard

Preparation time: 10 minutes

Cooking time: 8 hours

Servings: 6

Ingredients:

- 1 cup pumpkin, pureed

- 45 ounces canned black beans, drained

- 30 ounces canned tomatoes, chopped

- 1 yellow bell pepper, chopped

- 1 yellow onion, chopped

- ¼ teaspoon nutmeg, ground

- 1 teaspoon cinnamon powder

- 1 tablespoon chili powder

- 1 teaspoon cumin, ground

- 1/8 teaspoon cloves, ground

- A pinch of sea salt

- Black pepper to the taste

Directions:

1. Put pumpkin puree in your slow cooker.

2. Add black beans, tomatoes, onion, bell pepper, cumin, nutmeg, cinnamon, chili powder, cloves, salt and pepper, stir, cover and cook on Low for 8 hours.

3. Stir your chili again, divide into bowls and serve.

4. Enjoy!

Nutrition:

Calories: 242g,

Fat: 22g,

Carbs: 5g,

Protein: 34g,

13. **Crazy Cauliflower and Zucchini Surprise**

Difficulty: Hard

Preparation time: 10 minutes

Cooking time: 3 hours and 30 minutes

Servings: 4

Ingredients:

- 1 cauliflower head, florets separated

- 2 garlic cloves, minced

- ¾ cup red onion, chopped

- 1 teaspoon basil, dried

- 2 teaspoons oregano flakes

- 28 ounces canned tomatoes, chopped

- ¼ teaspoon red pepper flakes

- ½ cup veggie stock

- 5 zucchinis, cut with a spiralizer

- A pinch of salt

- Black pepper to the taste

Directions:

1. Put cauliflower florets in your slow cooker.

2. Add garlic, onion, basil, oregano, tomatoes, stock, pepper flakes, salt and pepper, stir, cover and cook on High for 3 hours and 30 minutes.

3. Mash cauliflower mix a bit using a masher.

4. Divide zucchini noodles in bowls, top each with cauliflower mix and serve.

5. Enjoy!

Nutrition:

Calories: 302g,

Fat: 22g,

Carbs: 5g,

Protein: 34g,

14. **Spaghetti Squash Bowls**

Difficulty: Hard

Preparation time: 10 minutes

Cooking time: 8 hours

Servings: 4

Ingredients:

- 5 pounds spaghetti squash, peeled

- 2 cups water

- 2 cups broccoli florets, steamed

- 1 tablespoon sesame seeds

- Chopped peanuts for serving

- ½ batch salad dressing

- For the salad dressing:

- 1 tablespoon palm sugar

- 1 tablespoon ginger, grated

- 3 tablespoons rice wine vinegar

- 3 tablespoons olive oil

- 2 tablespoons peanut butter

- 1 tablespoon soy sauce

- 3 garlic cloves, minced

- 1 teaspoon sesame oil

- ½ teaspoon sesame seeds

Directions:

1. In your blender, mix ginger with sugar, vinegar, oil, soy sauce, garlic, peanut butter, sesame oil and ½ teaspoon sesame seeds, pulse really well and leave aside.

2. Put the squash in your slow cooker, add the water, cover and cook on Low for 8 hours.

3. Leave squash to cool down, cut in halves, scrape flesh and transfer into a bowl.

4. Add broccoli florets, 1 tablespoon sesame seeds, chopped peanuts and the salad dressing.

5. Toss salad well and serve.

6. Enjoy!

Nutrition:

Calories: 102g,

Fat: 22g,

Carbs: 5g,

Protein: 34g,

15. **Mahi Mahi Taco Wraps**

Difficulty: Medium

Preparation Time: 5 Minutes

Cooking Time: 2 Hours **Servings:** 6

Ingredients:

- 1-pound Mahi Mahi, wild-caught

- ½ cup cherry tomatoes

- 1 small green bell pepper

- 1/4 of a medium red onion

- ½ teaspoon garlic powder

- 1 teaspoon sea salt

- ½ teaspoon ground black pepper

- 1 teaspoon chipotle pepper

- ½ teaspoon dried oregano

- 1 teaspoon cumin

- 2 tablespoons avocado oil

- 1/4 cup chicken stock

- 1 medium avocado, diced

- 1 cup sour cream

- 6 large lettuce leaves

Directions:

1. Grease a 6-quarts slow cooker with oil, place fish in it and then pour in chicken stock.

2. Stir together garlic powder, salt, black pepper, chipotle pepper, oregano and cumin and then season fish with half of this mixture.

3. Layer fish with tomatoes, pepper and onion, season with remaining spice mixture and shut with lid.

4. Plug in the slow cooker and cook fish for 2 hours at high heat setting or until cooked through.

5. When done, evenly spoon fish among lettuce, top with avocado and sour cream and serve.

Nutrition:

Net Carbs: 2g; Calories: 193.6; Total Fat: 12g; Saturated Fat: 1.7g;

Protein: 17g; Carbs: 5g; Fiber: 3g; Sugar: 2.5g

16. **Seafood Gumbo**

Difficulty: Medium

Preparation Time: 17 Minutes

Cooking Time: 2 Hours and 20 Minutes **Servings:** 6

Ingredients:

- 8 to 10 bacon strips, sliced

- 2 stalks celery, sliced

- 1 medium onion, sliced

- 1 green pepper, chopped

- 2 garlic cloves, minced

- 2 cups chicken broth

- 1 can (14 oz.) diced tomatoes, undrained

- 2 tbsp. Worcestershire sauce 2 tsp. salt

- 1 tsp. dried thyme leaves

- 1-pound large raw shrimp, peeled, deveined

- 1 pound fresh or frozen crabmeat

- 1 box (10 oz.) frozen okra, thawed and sliced into 1/2-inch

  pieces

Directions:

1. Brown the bacon in a skillet through medium heat. When crisp, drain and transfer to a slow cooker.

2. Drain off drippings, leaving just enough to coat the skillet.

3. Sauté celery, onion, green pepper, and garlic until vegetables are tender.

4. Transfer the sautéed vegetables to the slow cooker.

5. Add the broth, tomatoes, Worcestershire sauce, salt, and thyme.

6. Cover then cook it for 4 hours on LOW, or for 2 hours on HIGH.

7. Add the shrimp, crabmeat, and okra. Cover and cook 1 hour longer on LOW or 30 minutes longer on HIGH. Serve and enjoy!

Nutrition:

Calories 263, Fat 8, Carbs 13,

Protein 4

17. **Spinach and Olives Mix**

Difficulty: Very Easy

Preparation Time: 15 Minutes

Cooking Time: 3 Hours and 30 Minutes

Servings: 6

Ingredients:

- 2 cups spinach

- 2 tablespoons chives, chopped

- 5 oz Cheddar cheese, shredded

- ½ cup heavy cream

- 1 teaspoon ground black pepper

- ½ teaspoon salt

- 1 cup black olives, pitted and halved

- 1 teaspoon sage 1 teaspoon sweet paprika

Directions:

1. In the slow cooker, mix the spinach with the chives and the other ingredients, toss and close the lid.

2. Cook for 3.5 hours on Low and serve.

Nutrition:

Calories 189,

Fat 6.2,

Fiber 0.6,

Carbs 3,

Protein 3.4

18. **Aromatic Jalapeno Wings**

Difficulty: Medium

Preparation Time: 10 Minutes

Cooking Time: 3 Hours

Servings: 4

Ingredients:

- 1 jalapeño pepper, diced

- ½ cup of fresh cilantro, diced

- 3 tablespoon of coconut oil

- Juice from 1 lime

- 2 garlic cloves, peeled and minced

- Salt and black pepper ground, to taste

- 2 lbs. chicken wings Lime wedges, to serve

- Mayonnaise, to serve

Directions:

1. Start by throwing all the fixings into the large bowl and mix well.

2. Cover the wings and marinate them in the refrigerator for 2 hours.

3. Now add the wings along with their marinade into the Slow cooker.

4. Cover it and cook for 3 hours on Low Settings.

5. Garnish as desired.

6. Serve warm.

Nutrition:

Calories 246

Total Fat 7.4 g

Cholesterol 105 mg

Total Carbs 9.4 g

Sodium 353 mg

Potassium 529 mg

Protein 37.2 g

19. **Vegan Chickpeas Winter Mix**

Difficulty: Hard

Preparation time: 10 minutes

Cooking time: 4 hours and 10 minutes

Servings: 6

Ingredients:

- 1 yellow onion, chopped

- 1 tablespoon ginger, grated

- 1 tablespoon olive oil

- 4 garlic cloves, minced

- A pinch of salt and black pepper

- 2 red Thai chilies, chopped

- ½ teaspoon turmeric powder

- 2 tablespoons garam masala

- 4 ounces tomato paste

- 2 cups veggie stock

- 6 ounces canned chickpeas, drained

- 2 tablespoons cilantro, chopped

Directions:

1. Heat a pan with the oil over medium high heat, add ginger and onions, stir and cook for 4-5 minutes.

2. Add garlic, salt, pepper, Thai chilies, garam masala and turmeric, stir, cook for 2 minutes more and transfer everything to your slow cooker.

3. Add stock, chickpeas and tomato paste, stir, cover and cook on Low for 4 hours.

4. Add cilantro, stir, divide into bowls and serve. Enjoy!

Nutrition:

Calories 176, Fat 18.5, Fiber 3, Carbs 29.43,

Protein 23

20. **Curried Cauliflower**

Difficulty: Easy

Preparation Time: 10 Minutes

Cooking Time: 2 Hours and 30 Minutes

Servings: 4 to 5

Ingredients:

- 2 cups of medium cauliflower florets

- 1/3 cup tomato paste

- 1 tbsp

- 2 tbsp of olive oil

- 1 tsp of cumin

- 1 tbsp of curry

- 1 clove of garlic

- Salt Pepper

Directions:

1. Combine all the spices then season the cauliflower florets, making sure everything is covered evenly.

2. In a small dish, whisk together the tomato paste and mayo and spread over the cauliflower florets.

3. Set the slow cooker on high heat and cook the cauliflower for 2 ½ hours.

Nutrition:

Calories: 170,

Fat: 11g,

Carbs: 6g,

Protein: 6g

21. **Baked" Beans**

Difficulty: Very Hard

Preparation time: 10 minutes

Cooking time: 12 hours

Servings: 6

Ingredients:

- 1 pound navy beans, soaked overnight and drained

- 1 cup maple syrup

- 1 cup vegan BBQ sauce

- 4 tablespoons stevia

- 1 cup water

- ¼ cup tomato paste

- ¼ cup mustard

- ¼ cup olive oil

- ¼ cup apple cider vinegar

- 2 tablespoons coconut aminos

Directions:

1. In your slow cooker, mix beans with maple syrup, BBQ sauce, stevia, water, tomato paste, mustard, oil, vinegar and aminos, stir, cover and cook on Low for 12 hours.

2. Divide into bowls and serve hot.

3. Enjoy!

Nutrition:

Calories 576, Fat 18.5,

Fiber 3,

Carbs 29.43,

Protein 23

22. Squash Chili

Difficulty: Very Hard

Preparation time: 10 minutes

Cooking time: 6 hours Servings: 8

Ingredients:

- 2 carrots, chopped

- 1 yellow onion, chopped

- 2 celery stalks, chopped

- 2 green Papaya, cored, peeled and chopped

- 4 garlic cloves, minced

- 2 cups butternut squash, peeled and cubed

- 6 ounces canned chickpeas, drained

- 6 ounces canned black beans, drained

- 7 ounces canned coconut milk

- 2 teaspoons chili powder

- 1 teaspoon oregano, dried

- 1 tablespoon cumin, ground

- 2 cups veggie stock

- 2 tablespoons tomato paste

- Salt and black pepper to the taste

- 1 tablespoon cilantro, chopped

Directions:

1. In your slow cooker, mix carrots with onion, celery, Papaya, garlic, squash, chickpeas, black beans, coconut milk, chili powder, oregano, cumin, stock, tomato paste, salt and pepper, stir, cover and cook on High for 6 hours.

2. Add cilantro, stir, divide into bowls and serve.

3. Enjoy!

Nutrition:

Calories 376, Fat 18.5, Fiber 3, Carbs 29.43,

Protein 23 r

CHAPTER 5:

Dinner

23. **Moist and Spicy Pulled Chicken Breast**

Difficulty: Very Easy

Preparation time: 15 minutes

Cooking time: 6 hours

Servings: 8

Ingredients:

- 1 teaspoon dry oregano

- 1 teaspoon dry thyme

- 1 teaspoon dried rosemary

- 1 teaspoon garlic powder

- 1 teaspoon sweet paprika

- ½ teaspoon chili powder

- Salt and pepper to taste

- 4 tablespoons butter

- 1pounds of chicken breasts

- 1 ½ cups ready-made tomato salsa

- 2 Tablespoons of olive oil

Directions:

Mix dry seasoning, sprinkle half on the bottom of slow cooker.

Place the chicken breasts over it, sprinkle the rest of the spices.

Pour the salsa over the chicken. Cover, cook on low for 6 hours.

Nutrition:

Calories: 42

Carbs: 1g

Fat: 1g

Protein: 9g

24. **Whole Roasted Chicken**

Difficulty: Very Easy

Preparation time: 15 minutes

Cooking time: 8 hours

Servings: 6

Ingredients:

- 1 whole chicken (approximately 5.5 pounds)

- 4 garlic cloves

- 6 small onions

- 1 Tablespoon olive oil, for rubbing

- 2 teaspoons salt

- 2 teaspoons sweet paprika

- 1 teaspoon Cayenne pepper

- 1 teaspoon onion powder

- 1 teaspoon ground thyme

- 2 teaspoons fresh ground black pepper

- 4 Tablespoons butter, cut into cubes

Directions:

1. Mix all dry ingredients well.

2. Stuff the chicken belly with garlic and onions.

3. On the bottom of the slow cooker, place four balls of aluminum foil.

4. Set the chicken on top of the balls. Rub it generously with olive oil.

5. Cover the chicken with seasoning, drop in butter pieces. Cover, cook on low for 8 hours.

Nutrition:

Calories: 120

Carbs: 1g

Fat: 6g

Protein: 17g

25. **Pot Roast Beef Brisket**

Difficulty: Very Easy

Preparation time: 15 minutes

Cooking time: 12 hours Servings: 10

Ingredients:

- o pounds beef brisket, whole
- 2 Tablespoons olive oil
- 2 Tablespoons apple cider vinegar
- 1 teaspoon dry oregano
- 1 teaspoon dry thyme
- 1 teaspoon dried rosemary
- 2 Tablespoons paprika
- 1 teaspoon Cayenne pepper
- 1 tablespoon salt
- 1 teaspoon fresh ground black pepper

Directions:

1. In a bowl, mix dry seasoning, add olive oil, apple cider vinegar.

2. Place the meat in the slow cooker, generously coat with seasoning mix.

3. Cover, cook on low for 12 hours.

4. Remove the brisket, place it on a pan. Sear it under the broiler for 2-4 minutes, observe it, so the meat doesn't burn.

5. Wrap it using a foil, then let it rest for 1 hour. Slice and serve.

Nutrition:

Calories: 280

Carbs: 4g

Fat: 20g

Protein: 20g

26. **Seriously Delicious Lamb Roast**

Difficulty: Very Easy

Preparation time: 15 minutes

Cooking time: 8 hours

Servings: 8

Ingredients:

- 12 medium radishes, scrubbed, washed, and cut in half

- Salt and pepper to taste

- 1 red onion, diced

- 2 garlic cloves, minced

- 1 lamb joint (approximately 4.5 pounds) at room temperature

- 2 Tablespoons olive oil

- 1 teaspoon dry oregano

- 1 teaspoon dry thyme

- 1 sprig fresh rosemary

- 4 cups heated broth, your choice

Directions:

1. Place cut radishes along the bottom of the slow cooker. Season. Add onion and garlic.

2. Blend the herbs plus olive oil in a small bowl until it forms to paste.

3. Place the meat on top of the radishes. Knead the paste over the meat.

4. Heat the stock, pour it around the meat.

5. Cover, cook on low for 8 hours. Let it rest for 20 minutes. Slice and serve.

Nutrition:

Calories: 206

Carbs: 4g

Fat: 9g

Protein: 32g

27. **Lamb Provençal**

Difficulty: Very Easy

Preparation time: 15 minutes

Cooking time: 8 hours Servings: 4

Ingredients:

- 2 racks lamb, approximately 2 pounds

- 1 Tablespoon olive oil

- 2 Tablespoons fresh rosemary, chopped

- 1 Tablespoon fresh thyme, chopped

- 4 garlic cloves, minced

- 1 teaspoon dry oregano

- 1 lemon, the zest

- 1 teaspoon minced fresh ginger

- 1 cup (Good) red wine

- Salt and pepper to taste

Directions:

1. Preheat the slow cooker on low.

2. In a pan, heat 1 tablespoon olive oil. Brown the meat for 2 minutes per side.

3. Mix remaining ingredients in a bowl.

4. Place the lamb in the slow cooker, pour the remaining seasoning over the meat.

5. Cover, cook on low for 8 hours.

Nutrition:

Calories: 140

Carbs: 3g

Fat: 5g

Protein: 21g

28. **Garlic Lemon Sauce-less Ribs**

Difficulty: Hard

Preparation time: 15 minutes

Cooking time: 8 hours Servings: 4

Ingredients:

- 4 lb. pork ribs 2 T. garlic powder

- 2 T. sea salt 2 T. black pepper

- 1 T. cumin

- 3 lemons, juiced

Directions:

1. In a bowl, combine garlic powder, salt, pepper, and cumin. Rub spices over ribs, making sure to coat them thoroughly.

2. Put the ribs inside the slow cooker, then pour lemon juice over the ribs. Cook on low within 8 hours or on high within 5 hours.

Nutrition:

Calories: 287 Fats: 18 g Carbs: .5 g Fiber: 1 g

Protein: 29 g

29. **Garlic Dill Chicken Thighs**

Difficulty: Hard

Preparation time: 15 minutes

Cooking time: 4 hours

Servings: 4

Ingredients:

- 2 t. dried parsley

- 2 t. seasoned salt

- 1 ½ t. black pepper

- 1 t. garlic powder

- ½ t. dried dill

- ½ t. onion powder

- 8 boneless, skinless chicken thighs

- 6 oz pesto ½ c. chicken broth

Directions:

1. In a small bowl, combine spices. Arrange chicken in a slow cooker. Top with pesto, chicken broth, and spice mixture.

2. Stir to combine and thoroughly coat each piece of chicken. Cook on high within 3-4 hours.

Nutrition:

Calories: 456

Fats: 30 g

Carbs: 2 g

Fiber: 1 g

Protein: 47 g

30. **Oregano Italian Sausage Meatballs**

Difficulty: Hard

Preparation time: 15 minutes

Cooking time: 1 hour

Servings: 4

Ingredients:

- 1 ½ lb. ground beef

- 2 c. Alfredo sauce

- 5 pepper jack cheese slices

- 1 t. oregano

- 1 t. salt

- 1 ½ Italian sausage, spicy

- 1/3 c. pork rinds

- 2 eggs   1 t. Italian seasoning

Directions:

1. Combine all ingredients except Alfredo sauce. Form mixture into meatballs.

2. Put the meatballs inside the slow cooker and add Alfredo sauce. Set the slow cooker to LOW and cook for 1 hour.

3. Serve.

Nutrition:

Calories: 289

Fats: 22.6 g

Carbs: 1.2 g

Fiber: 1 g

Protein: 20.8 g

CHAPTER 6:

Vegan & Vegetarian

31. Homemade Vegetable Stock

Difficulty: Very Easy

Preparation time: 15 minutes

Cooking time: 12 hours & 30 minutes

Servings: 4

Ingredients:

- 4 quarts cold filtered water

- 12 whole peppercorns

- 3 peeled and chopped carrots

- 3 chopped celery stalks

- 2 bay leaves

- 4 smashed garlic cloves

- 1 large quartered onion

- 2 tablespoons apple cider vinegar

- Any other vegetable scraps

Directions:

1. Put everything in your slow cooker and cover. Do not turn on; let it sit for 30 minutes.

2. Cook on low for 12 hours. Strain the broth and discard the solids.

3. Before using, keep the stock in a container in the fridge for 2-3 hours.

Nutrition:

Calories: 11

Protein: 0g

Carbs: 3g

Fat: 0g

Fiber: 0g

32. **Cream of Zucchini Soup**

Difficulty: Very Easy

Preparation time: 15 minutes

Cooking time: 2 hours & 10 minutes

Servings: 4

Ingredients:

- 3 cups vegetable stock

- 2 pounds chopped zucchini

- 2 minced garlic cloves

- ¾ cup chopped onion

- ¼ cup basil leaves

- 1 tablespoon extra-virgin olive oil

- Salt and pepper to taste

Directions:

1. Heat-up olive oil in a skillet. When hot, cook garlic and onion for about 5 minutes.

2. Pour into your slow cooker with the rest of the fixings. Close the lid.

3. Cook on low for 2 hours. Puree the soup with an immersion blender. Serve.

Nutrition:

Calories: 96

Protein: 7g

Carbs: 11g

Fat: 5g

Fiber: 2.3g

33. **Tomato Soup**

Difficulty: Very Easy

Preparation time: 15 minutes

Cooking time: 4 hours

Servings: 4

Ingredients:

- 1 can crushed tomatoes

- 1 cup vegetable broth

- ½ cup heavy cream

- 2 tablespoons chopped parsley

- ½ teaspoon onion powder

- ½ teaspoon garlic powder

- Salt and pepper to taste

Directions:

1. Put all the fixings except heavy cream in the slow cooker, then cook on low for 4 hours.

2. Blend then stir in the cream using an immersion blender. Taste and season with more salt and pepper if necessary.

Nutrition:

Calories: 165

Protein: 3g Carbs: 15g

Fat: 13g Fiber: 3.7g

34. **Vegetable Korma**

Difficulty: Very Easy

Preparation time: 15 minutes

Cooking time: 8 hours Servings: 4

Ingredients:

- 1 head's worth of cauliflower florets

- ¾ can of full-fat coconut milk

- 2 cups chopped green beans

- ½ chopped onion

- 2 minced garlic cloves

- 2 tablespoons curry powder

- 2 tablespoons coconut flour

- 1 teaspoon garam masala

- Salt and pepper to taste

Directions:

1. Add vegetables into your slow cooker. Mix coconut milk with

   seasonings.

2. Pour into the slow cooker. Sprinkle over coconut flour and mix until blended.

3. Close and cook on low for 8 hours. Taste and season more if necessary. Serve!

Nutrition:

Calories: 206

Protein: 5g

Carbs: 18g

Fat: 14g

Fiber: 9.5g

35. **Zoodles with Cauliflower-Tomato Sauce**

Difficulty: Very Easy

Preparation time: 15 minutes

Cooking time: 3 hours & 31 minutes Servings: 4

Ingredients:

- 5 large spiralized zucchinis

- Two 24-ounce cans of diced tomatoes

- 2 small heads' worth of cauliflower florets

- 1 cup chopped sweet onion

- 4 minced garlic cloves

- ½ cup veggie broth

- 5 teaspoons Italian seasoning

- Salt and pepper to taste

- Enough water to cover zoodles

Directions:

1. Put everything but the zoodles into your slow cooker. Cook on high for 3 ½ hours.

2. Smash into a chunky sauce with a masher or another utensil.

3. To cook the zoodles, boil a large pot of water. When boiling, cook zoodles for just 1 minute, then drain—Season with salt and pepper. Serve sauce over zoodles!

Nutrition:

Calories: 113

Protein: 7g

Carbs: 22g

Fat: 2g

Fiber: 10.5g

36. **Spaghetti Squash Carbonara**

Difficulty: Very Easy

Preparation time: 15 minutes

Cooking time: 8 hours & 10 minutes Servings: 4

Ingredients:

- 2 cups of water

- One 3-pound spaghetti squash

- ½ cup coconut bacon

- ½ cup fresh spinach leaves

- 1 egg 3 tablespoons heavy cream

- 3 tablespoons unsweetened almond milk

- ½ cup grated Parmesan cheese

- 1 teaspoon garlic powder

- Salt and pepper to taste

Directions:

1. Put squash in your cooker and pour in 2 cups of water. Close the lid.

2. Cook on low for 8-9 hours. When the spaghetti squash cools, mix egg, cream, milk, and cheese in a bowl.

3. When the squash is cool enough for you to handle with oven mitts, cut it open lengthwise and scrape out noodles. Mix in the egg mixture right away.

4. Add spinach and seasonings. Top with coconut bacon and enjoy!

Nutrition:

Calories: 211

Protein: 5g

Carbs: 26g

Fat: 11g

Fiber: 5.1g

CHAPTER 7:

Desserts

37. Keto Coconut Hot Chocolate

Difficulty: Very Easy

Preparation time: 15 minutes

Cooking time: 4 hours

Servings: 8

Ingredients:

- 5 cups full-fat coconut milk

- 2 cups heavy cream

- 1 tsp vanilla extract

- 1/3 cup cocoa powder

- 3 ounces dark chocolate, roughly chopped

- ½ tsp cinnamon

- Few drops of stevia to taste

Directions:

1. Add the coconut milk, cream, vanilla extract, cocoa powder, chocolate, cinnamon, and stevia to the slow cooker and stir to combine.

2. Cook for 4 hours, high, whisking every 45 minutes.

3. Taste the hot chocolate and if you prefer more sweetness, add a few more drops of stevia.

Nutrition:

Calories: 135

Carbs: 5g

Fat: 11g

Protein: 5g

38. **Ambrosia**

Difficulty: Very Easy

Preparation time: 15 minutes

Cooking time: 3 hours Servings: 10

Ingredients:

- 1 cup unsweetened shredded coconut

- ¾ cup slivered almonds

- 3 ounces dark chocolate (high cocoa percentage), roughly chopped

- 1/3 cup pumpkin seeds

- 2 ounces salted butter

- 1 tsp cinnamon 2 cups heavy cream

- 2 cups full-fat Greek yogurt

- 1 cup fresh berries – strawberries and raspberries are best

Directions:

1. Place the shredded coconut, slivered almonds, dark chocolate, pumpkin seeds, butter, and cinnamon into the slow cooker.

2. Cook for 3 hours, high, stirring every 45 minutes to combine the chocolate and butter as it melts.

3. Remove the mixture from the slow cooker, place in a bowl, and leave to cool.

4. In a large bowl, whip the cream until softly whipped.

5. Stir the yogurt through the cream.

6. Slice the strawberries into pieces, then put it to the cream mixture, along with the other berries you are using, fold through.

7. Sprinkle the cooled coconut mixture over the cream mixture.

Nutrition:

Calories: 57

Carbs: 11g Fat: 1g

Protein: 1g

39. **Dark Chocolate and Peppermint Pots**

Difficulty: Very Easy

Preparation time: 15 minutes

Cooking time: 2 hours

Servings: 6

Ingredients:

- 2 ½ cups heavy cream

- 3 ounces dark chocolate, melted in the microwave

- 4 egg yolks, lightly beaten with a fork

- Few drops of stevia

- Few drops of peppermint essence to taste

Directions:

1. Mix the beaten egg yolks, cream, stevia, melted chocolate, and peppermint essence in a medium-sized bowl.

2. Prepare the pots by greasing 6 ramekins with butter.

3. Pour the chocolate mixture into the pots evenly.

4. Put the pots inside the slow cooker and put hot water below halfway up.

5. Cook for 2 hours, high. Take the pots out of the slow cooker and leave to cool and set.

6. Serve with a fresh mint leaf and whipped cream.

Nutrition:

Calories: 125

Carbs: 15g

Fat: 6g

Protein: 1g

40. **Creamy Vanilla Custard**

Difficulty: Very Easy

Preparation time: 15 minutes

Cooking time: 3 hours

Servings: 8

Ingredients:

- 3 cups full-fat cream

- 4 egg yolks, lightly beaten

- 2 tsp vanilla extract

- Few drops of stevia

Directions:

1. Mix the cream, egg yolks, vanilla extract, and stevia in a medium-sized bowl.

2. Pour the mixture into a heat-proof dish. Place the dish into the slow cooker.

3. Put hot water into the pot, around the dish, halfway up. Set the temperature to high.

4. Cook for 3 hours. Serve hot or cold!

Nutrition:

Calories: 206

Carbs: 30g

Fat: 7g

Protein: 6g

41. **Coconut, Chocolate, and Almond Truffle Bake**

Difficulty: Very Easy

Preparation time: 15 minutes

Cooking time: 4 hours Servings: 8

Ingredients:

- 3 ounces butter, melted

- 3 ounces dark chocolate, melted

- 1 cup ground almonds

- 1 cup desiccated coconut

- 3 tbsp. unsweetened cocoa powder

- 2 tsp vanilla extract

- 1 cup heavy cream

- A few extra squares of dark chocolate, grated

- ¼ cup toasted almonds, chopped

Directions:

1. In a large bowl, mix the melted butter, chocolate, ground almonds, coconut, cocoa powder, and vanilla extract.

2. Roll the mixture into balls. Grease a heat-proof dish.

3. Place the balls into the dish—Cook for 4 hours, low setting.

4. Leave the truffle dish to cool until warm. Mix the cream until soft peak.

5. Spread the cream over the truffle dish and sprinkle the grated chocolate and chopped toasted almonds over the top. Serve immediately!

Nutrition:

Calories: 115

Carbs: 8g

Fat: 10g

Protein: 2g

42. **Peanut Butter, Chocolate, and Pecan Cupcakes**

Difficulty: Very Easy

Preparation time: 15 minutes

Cooking time: 4 hours Servings: 14

Ingredients:

- 14 paper cupcake cases 1 cup smooth peanut butter

- 2 ounces butter 2 tsp vanilla extract

- 5 ounces dark chocolate

- 2 tbsp. coconut oil 2 eggs, lightly beaten

- 1 cup ground almonds

- 1 tsp baking powder 1 tsp cinnamon

- 10 pecan nuts, toasted and finely chopped

Directions:

1. Dissolve the dark chocolate plus coconut oil in the microwave, stir to combine, and set aside.

2. Place the peanut butter and butter into a medium-sized bowl, microwave for 30 seconds at a time until the butter has just

melted.

3. Mix the peanut butter plus butter until combined and smooth.

4. Stir the vanilla extract into the peanut butter mixture.

5. Mix the ground almonds, eggs, baking powder, and cinnamon in a small bowl.

6. Pour the melted chocolate and coconut oil evenly into the 14 paper cases.

7. Spoon half of the almond/egg mixture evenly into the cases, on top of the chocolate and press down slightly.

8. Spoon the peanut butter mixture into the cases, on top of the almond/egg mixture.

9. Spoon the remaining almond/egg mixture into the cases.

10. Put the pecans on top of each cupcake.

11. Put the filled cases into the slow cooker—Cook for 4 hours, high setting.

Nutrition:

Calories: 145 Carbs: 20g

Fat: 3g Protein: 4g

43. **Vanilla and Strawberry Cheesecake**

Difficulty: Very Easy

Preparation time: 15 minutes

Cooking time: 6 hours

Servings: 8

Ingredients:

- Base:
- 2 ounces butter, melted
- 1 cup ground hazelnuts
- ½ cup desiccated coconut
- 2 tsp vanilla extract
- 1 tsp cinnamon
- Filling:
- 2 cups cream cheese
- 2 eggs, lightly beaten
- 1 cup sour cream
- 2 tsp vanilla extract

- 8 large strawberries, chopped

Directions:

1. Mix the melted butter, hazelnuts, coconut, vanilla, and cinnamon in a medium-sized bowl.

2. Press the base into a greased heat-proof dish.

3. Mix the cream cheese, eggs, sour cream, and vanilla extract, beat with electric egg beaters in a large bowl until thick and combined.

4. Fold the strawberries through the cream cheese mixture.

5. Put the cream cheese batter into the dish, on top of the base, spread out until smooth.

6. Put it in the slow cooker and put hot water around the dish until halfway up.

7. Cook for 6 hours, low setting until just set but slightly wobbly.

8. Chill before serving.

Nutrition:

Calories: 156 Carbs: 4g

Fat: 7g Protein: 15g

44. Coffee Creams with Toasted Seed Crumble Topping

Difficulty: Easy

Preparation time: 15 minutes

Cooking time: 4 hours

Servings: 6

Ingredients:

- 2 cups heavy cream

- 3 egg yolks, lightly beaten

- 1 tsp vanilla extract

- 3 tbsp. strong espresso coffee (or 3tsp instant coffee dissolved in 3tbsp boiling water)

- ½ cup mixed seeds – sesame seeds, pumpkin seeds, chia seeds, sunflower seeds,

- 1 tsp cinnamon 1 tbsp. coconut oil

Directions:

1. Heat-up the coconut oil in a small frypan until melted.

2. Add the mixed seeds, cinnamon, and a pinch of salt, toss in the oil and heat until toasted and golden, place into a small bowl and set aside.

3. Mix the cream, egg yolks, vanilla, and coffee in a medium-sized bowl.

4. Pour the cream/coffee mixture into the ramekins.

5. Place the ramekins into the slow cooker. Put hot water inside until halfway.

6. Cook on low setting for 4 hours.

7. Remove, then leave to cool slightly on the bench.

8. Sprinkle the seed mixture over the top of each custard before serving.

Nutrition:

Calories: 35

Carbs: 4g

Fat: 2g

Protein: 1g

CHAPTER 8:

Poultry Recipes

45. **Cheese-Stuffed Turkey Meatballs**

Difficulty: Hard

Preparation time: 30 minutes

Cooking time: 5 hours 20 minutes

Servings: 5

Ingredients:

- 2 tbsp. Italian seasonings

- ½ c. of each:

- Grated parmesan cheese

- Rolled oats

- 2 eggs

- ½ t. of each:

- Pepper

- Salt

- Garlic powder

- 8 oz. Fontina cheese (24 pc.)

- 2 ½ lb. turkey

- *Marinara Sauce Ingredients*

- 1 can (28 oz.) crushed tomatoes

- 1 tbsp. EVOO (olive oil)

- ½ t. pepper

- 1 t. of each:

- Salt

- Dried parsley

- 2 t. of each:

- Dried basil

- Minced garlic

Directions:

1. Whisk the cheese, eggs, oats, and seasonings in a mixing container.

2. Fold in the turkey and roll into 24 meatballs.

3. Insert one tube of the cheese in the middle of each if the turkey meatballs.

4. Prepare the marinara sauce, and pour a layer into the cooker. Place the meatballs in the sauce, and stir in the remainder of the sauce.

5. Close the lid, and prepare for six hours using the lower setting or three hours using the highest temperature setting.

Nutrition:

Calories: 453, Fat: 39g, Carbs: 12g,

Protein: 14g.

46. **Chicken Legs**

Difficulty: Hard

Preparation time: 30 minutes

Cooking time: 1 hours 20 minutes

Servings: 5

Ingredients:

- 2 c. water

- 2 tbsp. swerve/15 drops stevia drops

- ¼ c. liquid aminos

- Optional: ¼ t. blackstrap molasses

- 1 t. of each:

- -Garlic powder

- -Ground ginger

- Pepper and salt to taste

- 6 ½ lb. chicken thighs & drumsticks

- Suggested: 6-quart slow cooker

Directions:

1. Mix the molasses, aminos, sweetener, garlic powder, water, and ground ginger. Cut the chicken up into pieces, and toss them into the pot.

2. Prepare the chicken on the high setting for five to six hrs. Or on the low setting for seven to eight hrs.

3. Serve and enjoy!

Nutrition:

Calories: 253,

Fat: 39g,

Carbs: 12g,

Protein: 14g.

CHAPTER 9:

Lamb & Beef Recipes

47. **Barbecue Lamb**

Difficulty: Hard

Preparation time: 30 minutes

Cooking time: 3 hours 20 minutes Servings: 5

Ingredients:

- ¼ c. dried mustard

- 5 ½ lbs. leg of lamb - boneless

- 2 tbsp. of each:

- -Smoked paprika

- Himalayan salt

- 1 tbsp. of each:

- Chipotle powder

- Dried oregano

- Ground cumin

- 1 c. water

Directions:

1. Combine the paprika, oregano, chipotle powder, cumin, and salt.

2. Cover the roast with the dried mustard, and sprinkle with the prepared spices. Arrange the lamb in the slow cooker, cover, and let it marinate in the refrigerator overnight. In the morning, let the pot come to room temperature. Once you're ready to cook, just add the cup of water to the slow cooker on the high heat setting. Cook for six hours.

3. When done, remove all except for one cup of the cooking juices, and shred the lamb. Using the rest of the cooking juices - adjust the seasoning as you desire, and serve

Nutrition:

Calories: 103, Fat: 19g, Carbs: 12g, Protein: 14g.

48. Lamb with Mint & Green Beans

Difficulty: Hard

Preparation time: 30 minutes

Cooking time: 6 hours 20 minutes

Servings: 2

Ingredients:

- ½ t. salt – Himalayan pink

- Freshly cracked black pepper

- 1 lamb leg – bone-in

- 2 tbsp. lard/ghee/tallow

- 4 garlic cloves

- 6 c. trimmed green beans

- ¼ freshly chopped mint/1-2 tbsp. dried mint

Directions:

1. Heat the slow cooker with the high setting.

2. Dry the lamb with some paper towels. Sprinkle with the pepper and salt. Grease a Dutch oven or similar large pot with the ghee/lard.

3. Sear the lamb until golden brown and set aside.

4. Remove the peels from the garlic and mince. Dice up the mint. Arrange the seared meat into the slow cooker and give it a shake of the garlic and mint.

5. Secure the lid and program the cooker on the low-heat function (10 hrs.) or the high-function (6 hrs.).

6. After about four hours, switch the lamb out of the cooker. Toss in the green beans and return the lamb back into the pot. Note: You can add ½ cup to one cup of water to the cooker if it gets dried out.

7. Let the flavors mingle for about two more hours. The meat should be tender and the beans crispy. Serve and enjoy!

Nutrition:

Calories: 180, Fat: 22g, Carbs: 7g, Protein: 15g.

CHAPTER 10:

Meat Recipes

49. Mild Chili Beef for Breakfast

Difficulty: Medium

Preparation time: 40 minutes

Cooking time: 3 ½ hours

Servings: 4

Ingredients:

- 2 oz of ground beef (with a 75/25% meat to fat ratio)

- 1 medium red onion, chopped

- 1 clove of garlic, minced

- 1 tbsp. of cumin

- 1 tbsp. of cayenne

- 1 tsp of paprika

- 1 cup of tomato juice

- 2 cups of vegetable stock

- 1 tbsp. of butter

- Salt/Pepper

Directions:

1. Lightly brown the ground beef with the onion and garlic using butter in a frying pan. Season with the spices and salt/pepper to taste.

2. Add to the slow cooker, cover with the stock and tomato juice, and give everything a good whisk.

3. Set to cook on low heat for 3 hours. Add optionally 1/3 cup shredded cheddar cheese on top over the last 20 minutes of cooking.

4. Serve with (optionally) coconut flour tortillas.

Nutrition:

Calories: 230, Fat: 11g, Carbs: 8g, Protein: 12g.

50. **Bacon and Spinach Frittata**

Difficulty: Hard

Preparation time: 30 minutes

Cooking time: 1 hours

Servings: 5

Ingredients:

- 5-6 strips of bacon, cooked

- 2 cups of fresh spinach leaves, washed and drained

- 8 large eggs, whisked

- ¼ cup heavy cream

- 1 cup of mozzarella cheese

- 1 tsp of Dill

- Salt

- Pepper

Directions:

1. Whisk all the ingredients together in a bowl.

2. Lightly grease the bottom of your slow cooker with butter and add all the ingredients.

3. Set and cook on high heat for 50 minutes.

Nutrition:

Calories: 270,

Fat: 20 g.

Carbs: 9 g.

Protein: 15g.

CHAPTER 11:

7 days Meal Plan

Days	Breakfast	Lunch	Dinner	Snacks
Day 1	Cherry Tomatoes Thyme Asparagus Frittata**Errore. Il segnalibro non è definito.**	Lemon Orzo	Moist and Spicy Pulled Chicken Breast	Keto Coconut Hot Chocolate
Day 2	Savory Creamy Breakfast Casserole	Lunch Sandwiches	Whole Roasted Chicken	Ambrosia
Day 3	Low-Carb Hash Brown Breakfast Casserole	Lunch Chicken Wraps	Pot Roast Beef Brisket	Dark Chocolate and Peppermint Pots
Day 4	Onion Broccoli Cream Cheese Quiche	Nutritious Lunch Wraps	Seriously Delicious Lamb Roast	Creamy Vanilla Custard
Day 5	Delicious Thyme Sausage Squash	Butternut Squash Soup	Lamb Provençal	Coconut, Chocolate, and Almond Truffle Bake

Day 6	Mexican Style Breakfast Casserole	Eggplant Bacon Wraps	Greek Style Lamb Shanks	Peanut Butter, Chocolate, and Pecan Cupcakes
Day 7	Cherry Tomatoes Thyme Asparagus Frittata	Mexican Warm Salad	Homemade Meatballs and Spaghetti Squash	Vanilla and Strawberry Cheesecake

Conclusion

When you shift to the ketogenic diet, it is essential to consider your overall health, just like any eating plan you need to maintain a healthy lifestyle to go with the diet. A healthy lifestyle is a choice. Just because we have thrown around the word "diet" does not mean that you should think of the ketogenic diet as something that only comes and goes. Suppose you choose to use this dietary plan. In that case, you need to remember that it is something you have to use not necessarily for the rest of your life. Still, you will have to incorporate many healthier aspects for the rest of your life if you want to stay healthy. It takes diligence to do this, but it is well worth it. When you start living a healthier life, you may want to start small by changing your regular meal plan to one of the slow cooker ketogenic recipes each day. Slow changes like this can help you too, within one or two weeks, switch over without as much pressure. Eventually, you can turn all of your meals into approved ones and if you miss a day or two don't knock yourself up. Like anything you choose to do, this takes time before your body fully adjusts.

If your objective is losing weight and get healthy by using the ketogenic diet, remember that weight loss has to include exercise. Even if you cut carbs out almost entirely and follow every facet of the ketogenic diet, you still need to exercise. Make exercise a daily habit of your new lifestyle just the same as making the food you regularly take a daily part of your lifestyle. Doing so will maximize all of your weight loss results.

What you need to know is that your body will respond to the demand that you put on it, and it will respond to the Keto food changes and exercise with time. If you ask your muscles to lift something heavy, it will get stronger and lift something heavy. If you ask your muscles to stay stagnant and sit on the couch, they will shrivel up and do exactly that.

Exercise damages your muscle which then allows your body to remodel the muscle to prevent further injury. Each time you train the small fibers, you injure them and force them to get bigger and stronger. It means that intense exercise is essential.

Your muscles respond to calories. Research shows that people who restrict their calories end up losing muscle mass with slower digestion or metabolism. Essential calorie restriction is not enough. It is necessary that you eat and that you eat well and exercise simultaneously.

The proteins and the fluid in your muscle fibers are broken down and rebuilt approximately every 7 to 15 days. Training can change this by impacting the type of proteins and the amount of protein your body produces.

Energy from your fat stores can be released and stored inside your muscle tissue, but you need ample nutrients and patience as this process takes place. Eating right is always the best way to go, and so is eating enough. Weight loss without proper calorie consumption is not something you should aim for.

Your hormones respond to exercise, and how they impact your weight loss depends heavily on your nutritional status, the number of calories you are consuming. Eating 2800 calories of pizza is not the same as 2800 calories of lean salmon and broccoli.

Your muscles (the ones that will help you burn fat or stay healthy) respond to calories. Research shows that people who restrict their calories to lose weight lose muscle mass with a slower metabolism. Simple calorie restriction is not enough. Some people who use stricter calories and field exercise ended up fatter than where they started. It is essential that you eat and that you eat well. It cannot be stress enough that you do need to enjoy lots of fats and lots of proteins with the keto diet. You cannot hope to generate the same amount of energy your body derives from simple carbohydrates if you do not make sure you are getting enough fat. Remember, fat is now your primary energy source so it should constitute a large part of your diet.

That said, you can reduce your carbohydrates quickly and make the change fast, or you can do it slowly and make the change gradually. As an athlete who wants to build muscle mass or better tone your body, you need to work hard enough for your body to burn off all the items included in the meal and make sure that you have high energy adequate to complete your workouts. You don't want to starve your body.

Remember the key to this particular diet is to get as many fats as you can.

Naturally, the time you spent eating out versus cooking at home is bound to change. When they switch to healthier diets, most people find that it is simply easier to have complete control over what you eat. You can never really trust a strange company to offer things how you like it nor can you be sure that they will have healthier choices. Eating out doesn't have to go away altogether, but the more you learn about the ketogenic diet, the more you can make wise choices when you have to attend things like company dinners or birthday events. Look up restaurant ahead of time and find out which ones serve the ketogenic friendly dish or at least have something that you can convert into a ketogenic friendly item.

CPSIA information can be obtained
at www.ICGtesting.com
Printed in the USA
BVHW050718160721
612048BV00012B/1069